MW00655101

▶ TRUTHS

about ABORTION

TEN TRUTHS ABOUT ABORTION

© 2007 Coral Ridge Ministries

All rights reserved. Written permission must be secured from the publisher to use or reproduce any part of this book, except for brief quotations in critical reviews or articles.

Published by Coral Ridge Ministries
Printed in the United States of America

All Scripture quotations, unless otherwise indicated, are taken from the New King James Version. Copyright © 1982 by Thomas Nelson, Inc. Used by permission. All rights reserved.

CORAL RIDGE MINISTRIES
Dr. D. James Kennedy, Founder

PROCLAIMING TRUTHS THAT
TRANSFORM THE WORLD

Post Office Box 40
Fort Lauderdale, Florida 33302
1-800-988-7884
www.coralridge.org
letters@coralridge.org

CONTENTS

CONTENTS

10▷ TRUTHS

about
ABORTION

(Newscom/Getty)

ABORTION IS ONE OF OUR NATION'S MOST
BITTERLY DISPUTED CONTROVERSIES.

INTRODUCTION

We have all heard the slogans and seen the signs:

"KEEP ABORTION LEGAL"

"ABORTION: THE ULTIMATE CHILD ABUSE"

"MY BODY, MY CHOICE"

"ABORTION KILLS CHILDREN"

Whether the discussion involves family members at the dinner table or tens of thousands of marching protesters, abortion is one of our nation's most bitterly disputed controversies. Some Americans believe that abortion is nothing less than the state-sanctioned slaughter of unborn babies. Others argue that it is a fundamental liberty guaranteed to all women.

Though abortion is often trumpeted as a giant stride forward in human freedom, Dr. D. James Kennedy, the founder of Coral Ridge Ministries, has rightly explained that abortion is a "great leap backward to ancient pagan practice … [and the rejection of] a 2,000-year-old Christian ethic that holds human life sacred."[1]

Greek and Roman cultures practiced abortion and eugenics. The weakest members of these societies were left on exposure walls to the wolves or worse. It wasn't until Christian ethics spread throughout the Western world that mercy and dignity were afforded to *all* human beings, from conception to death.

One cannot claim to revere human life and shrug at abortion. Even abortion proponents now admit that abortion equates to killing. In 1997, Faye Wattleton, former president of Planned

Parenthood (the nation's largest abortion provider), frankly admitted to *Ms.* magazine: "I think we have deluded ourselves into believing that people don't know that abortion is killing."

Indeed, polls show that a growing number of Americans are taking a negative view of abortion. A 2006 Zogby poll discovered a "sharp decline" in support for abortion, "The numbers were radically different ten years ago . . . maybe just seven or eight years ago," pollster John Zogby marveled.[2] The *Los Angeles Times* reported that 57 percent of Americans believe that "abortion is murder,"[3] and Gallup found that 72 percent of America's teens now believe abortion to be "morally unacceptable."[4]

Most Doctors Object to Abortion

A survey published in *The New England Journal of Medicine* revealed that most doctors also object to abortion.[5] The number of abortion providers has plummeted 37 percent since 1982,[6] causing the National Abortion Federation to complain that "access to abortion has been severely eroded."[7] This shift in popular opinion is life-saving. Between 1990 and 2002, the number of annual abortions declined by nearly 20 percent—representing more than 2.5 million infants who were allowed to live.[8]

More than twenty years ago, Dr. Kennedy predicted: "Eventually the hideous blot of legal abortion will be wiped away.... However, it will leave a scar on the historical character of our nation. It will shock our children that we could have allowed such a slaughter."[9]

✦ *Dr. D. James Kennedy*

If an unborn baby is a living human being, then Americans must come face-to-face with the fact that they have allowed a holocaust of unspeakable proportions. Just imagine if the entire populations of Arizona, Arkansas, Colorado, Idaho, Iowa, Kansas, Minnesota, Missouri, Montana, Nebraska, Nevada, New Mexico, North Dakota, Oregon, South Dakota, Utah, and Wyoming—over 47 million people—were totally wiped out with no survivors! Such a catastrophe would still fall short of the staggering death toll from abortion since 1973.

How to Read This Booklet

Those of you reading this booklet will, generally speaking, fall into one of three mindsets. Many of you consider yourselves "pro-life." **Ten Truths About Abortion** is designed to provide you with compelling, easily understood facts that will help you convince your friends, neighbors, and co-workers that abortion truly is a hideous blot on our national character.

One of the most powerful ways you can contribute is to win what we call "The Battle at the Water Cooler." Most of us engage in casual conversations during the work day or in other social settings. When these chats veer into the hot-button cultural issues of the day, it is often the person who is most passionate about the issue who dominates the discussion. Sadly, many of us remain silent at these times— in part, because we do not wish to ignite a furious debate, but often because we feel ill-equipped to answer the arguments that may be thrown at us.

Each of the ten truths in this little booklet can be absorbed quickly and easily, equipping you to explain why abortion is never a good idea for mother or child. One of the most common techniques taught to sales professionals has been referred to as the "Feel-Felt-Found" technique. A woman standing at the water cooler might argue, "It's my body; I have the right to do what I want with my own body." This provides you with the perfect opportunity to reply, "I know how you **feel**. I **felt** the same way, until I **found** out that…" Then—gently, patiently, and with humility—you share one of the ten truths contained in this booklet.

However, there is a second group of people reading **Ten Truths About Abortion** who do *not* call themselves "pro-life." In fact, you may not have any strong feelings about this issue one way or another. You may be wondering what all the fuss is about. You reason that a woman's "right to choose" abortion has been the law of our land for more than thirty years; why do Christians and social conservatives still debate the issue? This booklet will take only a few moments to read, but when you have finished, you will know why so many feel so strongly about this issue.

If You're "Pro-Choice"

Finally, some readers would describe themselves as "pro-choice." You believe that our United States Constitution guarantees the right to abortion. Perhaps a friend or family member gave you this booklet; perhaps you are just curious to see what kind of arguments "the other side" is offering. Please continue to read. We assure you at the outset that this booklet was written to inform, not to condemn. If you are fair-minded and willing to consider a different viewpoint, we believe you will no longer see this issue in the same way after learning the **Ten Truths About Abortion**.

Regardless of your mindset at the outset of this journey, you can read this booklet in little more time than you spend taking a shower each morning. You will see from the dozens of endnotes provided that we are not merely voicing our opinion; we are laying out the facts. We are sharing ten truths about abortion.

If you finish reading and want to learn more, please visit our website, www.coralridge.org and click on the "Equip and Grow" tab, or call us at 800-229-WORD (9673). We have several resources to help you develop a more in-depth understanding of this subject, including a DVD which was produced as a companion to this booklet.

Thank you for being willing to share your time with us. May God bless you as you pursue the truth about abortion.

TRUTH 1

**It Is a Proven Fact:
Life Begins at Conception**

If you are alive and breathing and reading this booklet, you once existed as a one-day-old embryo. You were not a "pre-human" mishap. Even your day-old DNA declared your humanity!

Sixty prominent physicians made that point with great clarity when they issued a declaration in defense of the unborn in the 1980s. The group included Bernard Nathanson, a former abortionist and co-founder of NARAL, a powerful pro-abortion organization; two past presidents of the American College of Obstetrics and Gynecology; and the former president of the American Academy of Neurology.

In their treatise, which was sent to President Ronald Reagan, they stated:

The developing fetus is not a sub-human species with a different genetic composition.... [T]he embryo is alive, human, and unique in the special environmental support required for that stage of human development.

○ *Infant seven weeks from conception (Life Issues Institute)*

The American College of Pediatricians agrees, declaring in its 2004 official policy statement that it "concurs with the body of scientific evidence that human life begins at conception—fertilization.... Scientific and medical discoveries over the past three decades [since *Roe v. Wade*] have only verified and solidified this age-old truth."[10]

Timeline for Life

Nevertheless, abortion advocates continue to insist that abortion destroys nothing more than clumps of cells or excess tissue. Such arguments can and should be summarily rejected. Here is a timeline of a baby's development during the first trimester of pregnancy:

CONCEPTION:	The baby's DNA (a complete genetic blueprint) is established. This determines the baby's gender, hair color, eye color, skin tone, height, and more.
18 DAYS:	*The heart begins to beat.*
19 DAYS:	*The baby's eyes begin to develop.*
FOUR WEEKS:	*Arms and legs begin to develop.*
FIVE WEEKS:	*The baby's mouth, ears, and nose are taking shape.*
SIX WEEKS:	*The baby kicks and has measurable brain waves.(A majority of abortions occur after the seventh week of gestation.)*
EIGHT WEEKS:	*All body systems are present. The baby sucks his thumb and responds to touch.*
TEN WEEKS:	*The structure of the baby's entire body is formed, even fingerprints and eyelashes.*
ELEVEN WEEKS:	*The baby's organ systems are complete and functioning. The baby breathes, swallows, digests, sleeps, tastes, hears, and hiccups.*

As you can see from the timeline, the slogan "Abortion Stops a Beating Heart" is entirely accurate. We are not discussing the surgical removal of a "clump of tissue." Abortion is the killing of an unborn human being. The unborn child is a human life from the moment of conception, and that life ends violently, often painfully (as you will see in the next section), on the abortionist's table.

The entire pro-abortion position hinges on denying the humanity of the unborn. If the supporters of legal abortion were to admit that human life begins at conception, they would be confronted with the fact that abortion is murder.

○ *Infant eleven weeks*
  from conception
  (Life Issues Institute)

The Ayn Rand Institute, a pro-abortion organization, conceded:

[A]bortion-rights advocates keep hiding behind the phrase "a woman's right to choose." Does she have the right to choose murder? That's what abortion would be, if the fetus were a person. The status of the embryo in the first trimester is the basic issue that cannot be sidestepped. The embryo is clearly pre-human; only the mystical notions of religious dogma treat this clump of cells as constituting a person.[11]

Pro-abortion advocates stubbornly refuse to acknowledge the humanity of the child in the womb. The Supreme Court took a similar position in 1973, when it issued the *Roe v. Wade* decision, which swept away all state and federal laws prohibiting abortion. The Court ruled that "the word 'person,' as used in the Fourteenth Amendment, does not include the unborn."[12]

Human From the Get-Go

Thirty years later, we know better. Attributing humanity to the unborn can no longer be brushed off as "mystical notions of religious dogma." To the contrary, it is a widely accepted scientific fact. After reviewing mounds of evidence, one U.S. Senate committee declared:

physicians, biologists, and other scientists agree

> that conception … marks the beginning of a human being—a being that is alive and is a member of the human species. There is overwhelming agreement on this point in countless medical, biological, and scientific writings.[13]

THE FACTS ARE INCONTROVERTIBLE;
*the unborn child in the womb
is a human child.*

TRUTH 2

**An Aborted Baby Dies a
Violent, Painful Death**

Dr. McArthur Hill, who performed first trimester abortions, confessed, "I have taken the lives of innocent babies, and I have ripped them from their mother's wombs with a powerful suction machine…. There isn't any way that you can say that there isn't a human body inside of those containers when you can look and see the little arms, feet, and faces."[14]

Dr. David Brewer spoke about his experience doing saline abortions, in which a baby is chemically burned to death. "[S]he was going to pieces; she was having a nervous breakdown, screaming and thrashing…. I walked in, and here was her little saline abortion baby kicking. It had been born alive, and was kicking and moving for a little while before it finally died of those terrible burns, because the salt solution gets into the lungs and burns the lungs, too."[15]

What Abortionists Do

In recounting a dilation and evacuation abortion, Dr. Anthony Levantino explained, "[A]s a doctor, you are sitting there tearing, and I mean tearing—you need a lot of strength to do it—arms and legs off of babies and putting them in a stack on top of the table."

✝ Forceps: This abortion tool is used to crush, grasp, and pull the child's body apart. (Grantham Collection)

One nurse who participated in a late-term abortion recalled, "The baby's little fingers were clasping and unclasping, and his little feet were kicking. Then the doctor stuck the scissors in

the back of his head, and the baby's arms jerked out …
The doctor opened up the scissors, stuck a high-powered suction tube into the opening and sucked the baby's brains out. Now the baby went completely limp."[16]

Even the most graphic descriptions fall short of capturing the sheer brutality of an abortion procedure. Carol Everett, a former abortion clinic owner, told an audience, "There are no words to describe how bad it really is."[17]

Abortion proponents cloak the various procedures used to end the baby's life in bland clinical terms, seeking to make the matter more palatable to the public. However, when you read the grotesque details of what actually happens behind clinic doors, it is impossible to minimize the horror. The procedure is not a neat surgical extraction of excess tissue; it is the violent dismemberment of a defenseless baby.

After reviewing testimonies involving just one method of abortion, Supreme Court Justice Antonin Scalia wrote, **"The method of killing a human child … is so horrible that the most clinical description of it evokes a shudder of revulsion."**[18]

➥ *Antonin Scalia*
(Newscom/Getty)

The horrific nature of abortion is only compounded by the mounting evidence that unborn babies are sensitive to touch and pain. After reviewing testimony offered to a congressional committee, Senator Sam Brownback told fellow senators, "We now know that unborn children can not only feel, but that their ability to experience pain is heightened. The highest density of pain receptors per square inch of skin in human development occurs in utero from 20 to 30 weeks gestation."[19]

Dr. Steven Calvin, perinatologist at the University of Minnesota, explained that "neural pathways are present for pain to be experienced quite early by unborn babies."[20]

"Severe and Excruciating" Pain

Dr. Kanwaljeet Anand, a pediatrician from the University of Arkansas, testified that babies suffer "severe and excruciating" pain during second and third trimester abortions.[21]

Many mothers can tell you stories about the reactions of their unborn children to stimuli from outside the womb—voices, sounds, pressure, and movement. One expectant mother, for example, recalled how the child within her jumped at the sound of a slamming door. Are we so naïve as to believe that these same babies are numb to the sharp, gleaming instruments of the abortionist?

The powerful movie, *The Silent Scream,* used ultrasound technology to film an actual abortion. The procedure was narrated by an experienced abortionist:

> [T]his suction tip which you can see moving violently back and forth on the bottom of the screen is the lethal instrument which will ultimately tear apart and destroy the child.... Now the child's heart rate has speeded up dramatically. And the child's movements are violent at this point. It does sense aggression in its sanctuary. It is moving away ... one can see it moving to the left side of the uterus... in an attempt ... a pathetic attempt to escape the inextricable instruments which the abortionist is using to extinguish its life.[22]

In a sermon titled "The American Holocaust," Dr. Kennedy discussed how deceptive euphemisms—words like "women's rights" and "reproductive health"—create a façade for an evil comparable to Nazi war crimes:

IN THE NUREMBERG TRIALS the Nazis were denounced for killing people in their gas chambers, for aborting children in their concentration camps and killing them…. Malcolm Muggeridge says something which I think is very interesting. He said, "Surely some future Gibbon, surveying our times will note sardonically that it took no more than three decades to transform a war crime into an act of compassion…"

Babies suffer "severe and excruciating" pain during abortions
(Newscom)

WE cannot—we must not—mince words on this subject.

The truth about abortion is that it subjects a living human being to a grotesque, often excruciating death.

TRUTH 3

**Abortion Hurts Women—
Now and in the Future**

Abortion not only destroys unborn babies, it scars women—physically and emotionally.

"Abortion hurts, deceives, and destroys," wrote Julie from Georgia. "I was not told about the possible physical health risks, lifetime of depression, fear, anxiety, grief, guilt, and remorse or shame. I was not told of complications that could cause infertility."[23]

Tami from Wyoming submitted an affidavit to the U.S. Supreme Court describing her "severe problems with reproductive organs, scarring, bleeding, infertility, depression, pain" subsequent to her abortion.

Thousands of similar affidavits have been collected from post-abortive women. Numerous studies show that women who have undergone an abortion suffer an increased risk of depression, substance abuse, alcohol abuse, suicide, infertility, premature delivery, ectopic pregnancy, miscarriages, stillbirths, sexual dysfunction, cervical cancer, ovarian cancer, and breast cancer.[24]

Despite the tremendous risks associated with abortion, more than one-third of American women will undergo one by the time they are 45.[25] Few will be told the truth about the potential physical and emotional devastation.

Abortion remains one of the least regulated of all medical fields. Dr. Warren Hern, a well-known abortionist and author of the medical textbook *Abortion Practice*, has acknowledged, "[T]here are few surgical procedures given so little attention and so underrated in its potential hazard as abortion."

Dr. Anthony Levatino, a former abortionist turned pro-life activist, admitted, "I have perforated uteruses. I have had all kinds of problems—bleeding, infection. Lord knows how many of those women are sterile now."[26]

Abortion and Premature Death

The dangers of abortion are not limited to disease, depression, and addiction; abortion has also been linked to premature death. One study published in the *Southern Medical Journal* involving more than 137,000 pregnant women found that those who chose abortion were 62 percent more likely to die within eight years of the procedure than those who delivered a live baby. Researchers attributed this heightened mortality rate to increased incidences of suicide, accidents, and disease. A similar Finnish study found that post-abortive women were 252 percent more likely to die within one year of their abortion than those who gave birth.[27]

In 2005, the South Dakota Legislature created a commission to study the impacts of abortion. After reviewing the testimony of 1,940 post-abortive women, the commission explained:

> **Women were not told the truth about abortion, were misled into thinking that nothing but "tissue" was being removed, and relate that they would not have had an abortion if they were told the truth. They almost uniformly**

express anger toward the abortion providers, their baby's father, or society in general, which promote abortion as a great right ... They are stunned by their grief and the negative impact it has had on their lives.[28]

△ Ellen Burstyn
(Newscom)

Academy Award-winning actress Ellen Burstyn told a radio interviewer in 2007 that having an abortion was the lowest point in her life. The movie star said it was "an extremely painful experience" that happened when she said she was "young and dumb" and didn't want to have a baby. But, "It was the wrong thing to do and I really didn't understand that 'til later," she said. "That was very, very painful. That was probably the worst." [29]

The U.S. Supreme Court has conceded that a post-abortive woman is often forced to "struggle with grief more anguished and sorrow more profound when she learns, only after the event, what she once did not know...."[30]

"I Wish I Had Known"

Bottom line: abortion hurts women. For every activist stridently defending a woman's "right to choose," there are many more broken voices crying, "I wish I had known how much misery I would live in because of it."[31]

In an affidavit pleading with the High Court to overturn *Roe v. Wade*, Caroline from Florida confessed,

> [Abortion] took my innocence. Robbed me of self-worth. Really made me numb. Alcohol use. Suicidal thoughts. Depression, anxiety. Unbelievable guilt. Shut my emotions down. I thought it would be over after one day, but fifteen years later, I'm still haunted by the memories and the tremendous guilt of ... having robbed my children of life. I still feel like I'm going to vomit when certain thoughts surface.[32]

U.S Supreme Court

THE U.S. SUPREME COURT
has conceded that a post-abortive woman is often forced to "struggle with grief more anguished and sorrow more profound when she learns, only after the event, what she once did not know…."[30]

TRUTH 4

**The Pro-Abortion Movement
Was Built on Lies and Deception**

Dr. Kennedy once declared, "Every evil system is based upon a foundation of lies." Such is the case with abortion. The entire pro-abortion movement was founded upon lies and more lies.

In the 1960s, the National Association for the Repeal of Abortion Laws (NARAL) launched a campaign to overturn all laws prohibiting abortion. Bernard Nathanson, co-founder of NARAL, now readily admits that the group's members lied in order to gain media attention. "We simply fabricated the results of fictional polls," he stated. "We announced to the media that we had taken polls and that 60 percent of Americans were in favor of permissive abortion." [33]

"Back-Alley" Myth

In addition, Nathanson, who is now pro-life, acknowledged that leaders of the early abortion movement grossly exaggerated claims about women dying in "back-alley" abortions. During a luncheon with Dr. Kennedy, Nathanson confirmed that the vast majority of abortions performed prior to 1973 were not done with coat hangers in back alleys, as pro-abortion activists frequently insist. Rather, they were performed by unscrupulous doctors who couldn't make a decent living in legitimate medical practice. [34] Nevertheless, NARAL continued promoting this lie to the media. Nathanson explained,

> Repeating the big lie often enough convinces the public. The number of women dying from illegal abortions was around

> 200-250 annually. The figure we constantly
> fed to the media was 10,000. These false
> figures took root in the consciousness
> of Americans, convincing many that
> we needed to crack the abortion law.[35]

That is exactly what happened. With crafty lies and clever slogans, NARAL quickly changed the tone of public debate. "I remember laughing when we made those slogans up," recalled Nathanson.

The lies did not stop. The two 1973 U.S. Supreme Court decisions that served to legalize abortion through all nine months of pregnancy—*Roe v. Wade* and *Doe v. Bolton*—were also founded upon outright deceit.

Roe Based on a Lie

Norma McCorvey, the unnamed plaintiff in *Roe*, confessed that her entire case "was all based on a lie." After abandoning her pro-abortion beliefs, McCorvey launched "*Roe* No More Ministries" and dedicated her life to overturning *Roe v. Wade*. In a letter to fellow Americans, she wrote:

> I owe you an apology. I said I was gang
> raped. And I wasn't. I said I didn't know
> who the father of my baby was. And I did. I
> said I wanted someone to kill my baby. And
> what I really wanted was someone to help
> me. It was a nasty, bald-faced lie. And I
> knew it…. For years abortion was my life,
> but the day-to-day stress of helping kill
> babies was eating away at my soul.[36]

Doe v. Bolton, which legalized abortion all the way to the point of delivery, was based upon another series of lies. Sandra Cano enlisted the help of an attorney, Margie Pitts Hames, to regain custody of her children. Without Cano's permission, Hames then filed a federal lawsuit—using Sandra as an anonymous plaintiff—to legalize abortion.

In 2000, in hopes of overturning *Doe v. Bolton*, Sandra Cano submitted an affidavit, explaining,

[I was] seeking custody of my children and a divorce from my husband. What I received was something I never requested—the legal right to abort my child…. I never wanted an abortion; I just wanted my children back…. The facts stated in the affidavit in *Doe v. Bolton* are not true…. *Doe v. Bolton* was fraud. It's based on fraud, and I'm a victim. I did not want abortion. I do not believe in it.[37]

○ *Now Pro-Life: From left, Sandra Cano, Dr. Bernard Nathanson and Norma McCorvey*

Both *Roe* and *Doe* were founded on a web of falsehood and deceit. It is interesting and encouraging to note that Bernard Nathanson, Norma McCorvey, and Sandra Cano are now all actively working to promote the right to life of unborn children. Nathanson produced two gripping pro-life documentaries, The *Silent Scream* and *The Eclipse of Reason*. Tragically, however, the pro-death movement that began with outright lies and deceptions continues to employ the same false and fraudulent information today. The light of truth is needed to dispel the dark and deceitful arguments used for abortion.

TRUTH 5

The "Right" to Abortion Is Not in the U.S. Constitution

On January 22, 1973, with one swing of the gavel, the U.S. Supreme Court gave women the right to snuff out the life of their unborn children. The Court's Roe v. Wade decision ignored the will of the American people and catapulted our nation into an era of bitter political division and moral decline.

In *Roe*, seven justices, with no experience in science or medicine, determined that unborn children were not entitled to any protection under the law. After citing examples from ancient pagan cultures, the Court asserted that "the unborn have never been recognized in the law as persons." However, in a private letter, Justice Harry Blackmun, author of the *Roe* decision, explained, "If this suggestion of personhood is established, the appellant's [pro-abortion] case, of course, collapses, for the fetus' right to life is then guaranteed…"

◢ *Harry Blackmun (Newscom)*

Decades later, medical science has conclusively established the humanity and personhood of the unborn, but the U.S. Supreme Court has refused to reverse its ruling.

In 2004, Judge Edith Jones, of the Fifth U.S. Circuit Court of Appeals, sharply criticized the *Roe* decision. In her conclusion, Jones wrote,

It takes no expert prognosticator to know that research on women's mental and physical health following abortion will yield an eventual medical consensus, and neonatal science will push the frontiers of fetal "viability" ever closer to the date of conception. One may fervently hope that the Court will someday acknowledge such developments and re-evaluate *Roe* and *Casey* accordingly.[38]

Several Supreme Court Justices have opposed the *Roe* decision. "The Constitution contains no right to abortion," Justice Antonin Scalia argued. "It is not to be found in the longstanding traditions of our society, nor can it be logically deduced from the text of the Constitution."[39]

Right to Life in Declaration, Constitution

Indeed, both the Declaration of Independence and the U.S. Constitution place tremendous emphasis on our God-given right to life. Most Americans are familiar with the Declaration's assertion: "We hold these truths to be self-evident, that all men are created equal, that they are endowed by their Creator with certain unalienable Rights, that among these are Life, Liberty and the pursuit of Happiness." In addition, the Fifth and Fourteenth Amendments to the U.S. Constitution promise that no person shall be deprived of life without due process of law. Indeed, many legal scholars believe that *Roe* was wrongly decided—including some of the most ardent advocates for legal abortion. Supreme Court Justice Ruth Bader Ginsburg described *Roe* as "heavy-handed judicial intervention" that remains "difficult to justify." Alan Dershowitz, a well-known pro-abortion Harvard law professor, labeled *Roe* an example of "judicial activism."[40] Laurence Tribe, professor of constitutional law at Harvard, stated, "Behind its own verbal smokescreen, the substantive judgment on which [*Roe*] rests is nowhere to be found."[41]

Edward Lazarus, who clerked for Justice Blackmun, admitted that "*Roe* borders on the indefensible" and called his mentor's decision a "jurisprudential nightmare" that "required an analytical leap with little support in history or precedent."[42]

Scar on Nation

While the right to abortion is nowhere to be found in the U.S. Constitution, the landmark case of *Roe v. Wade* has certainly scarred our national character. Mother Teresa once said reprovingly, "America needs no words from me to see how your decision in *Roe v. Wade* has deformed a great nation. The so-called right to abortion has pitted mothers against their children and women against men. It has portrayed the greatest of gifts—a child—as a competitor, an intrusion, and an inconvenience."

○ *Mother Teresa
(Newscom)*

In 1983, President Ronald Reagan
penned an essay titled "Abortion and the Conscience
of a Nation." In that pro-life tract, he wrote:

○ *Ronald Reagan*

Our nationwide policy of abortion-on-demand through all nine months of pregnancy was neither voted for by our people nor enacted by our legislators—not a single state had such unrestricted abortion before the Supreme Court decreed it to be national policy in 1973...

Make no mistake, abortion-on-demand is not a right granted by the Constitution. No serious scholar, including one disposed to agree with the Court's result, has argued that the framers of the Constitution intended to create such a right. ... Nowhere do the plain words of the Constitution even hint at a "right" so sweeping as to permit abortion up to the time the child is ready to be born. Yet that is what the Court ruled.

The High Court's ruling in Roe, Reagan wrote, in words that echoed former Supreme Court Justice Byron White, is nothing less than

"an act of raw judicial power."

TRUTH 6

Abortion Is Big Business and Big Bucks.

The abortion industry is making a bloody fortune. Each year, there are more than one million abortions performed in the United States. The Alan Guttmacher Institute, a research affiliate of Planned Parenthood, estimated in 2001 that the average cost per abortion was $487.[43]

"You can make a lot of money doing abortions," revealed **Anthony Levantino,** a former abortion provider. "In my practice, we were averaging between $250 and $500 per abortion [in the 1980s]—and it was cash. It is the one time as a doctor you can say, 'Either pay me up front or I'm not going to take care of you…. Either you have the money or you don't.'"[44]

Former abortion clinic owner Carol Everett was asked, " What is the governing force behind the abortion industry?"

It's About Money

"Money," **Everett answered bluntly. "It's a very lucrative business."**[45]

↙ *Carol Everett*

Norma McCorvey, who was the "Jane Roe" of *Roe v. Wade,* recalled her experience working in an abortion clinic. "It was just a racket," she said. "[The doctor] was just doing it for the money. He didn't care about the women…."[46]

Pro-abortion activists trumpet the importance of the so-called "right to choose," yet virtually all accounts show that the abortion industry is not interested in providing women with alternatives; they are interested in profits. Debra Henry, who worked as an assistant at an abortion clinic, remembers, "The women were *never* given any type of alternatives to abortions."

Nita Whitten worked as a secretary for a Dallas abortion clinic. "I was trained by a professional marketing director in how to sell abortions over the telephone," she recounted. "The object was, when the girl called, to hook the sale so she wouldn't get an abortion somewhere else, or adopt out her baby, or change her mind. We were doing it for the money."[47]

Some abortionists are more profitable than others.

The Planned Parenthood Federation of America (PPFA) is the nation's largest abortion provider. From 1997 to 2005, its clinics performed 1,918,532 surgical abortions.[48,49,50]

The organization is tremendously successful at marketing abortions. Even as the nation's annual abortion rate fell, the number of abortions performed by PPFA clinics rose more than sixty percent.

In 2005 alone, Planned Parenthood abortion clinics ended the lives of 264,943 unborn babies—which lays a death toll at the feet of this organization greater than all the lives lost in the previous year to breast cancer, diabetes, HIV/AIDS, homicide, leukemia, melanoma, ovarian cancer, prostate cancer, and suicide *combined*.[51,52] When D. James Kennedy called abortion "The American Holocaust," he was not exaggerating in the least.

Tax Dollars to Planned Parenthood

From 1997 to 2005, Planned Parenthood's own annual reports reveal that the abortion industry behemoth netted profits in excess of $469 million. During this same time period, the organization collected $2.07 billion from American taxpayers in government grants and contracts.

Incredibly, taxpayer funding for PPFA has nearly doubled since 1998. Though our nation is trillions of dollars in debt, many elected officials fight doggedly to maintain—and even increase—funding for abortion providers. Seventeen states actually allocate tax dollars specifically to help pay for the abortions of impoverished women.[53] If you pay taxes, you are helping to fill the financial coffers of America's abortion providers.

Never forget: Abortion is a moneymaking industry, a hugely profitable business that aggressively seeks to maintain its margins. Whether its funding comes from unsuspecting taxpayers or confused young women, the destruction of unborn life is a highly lucrative practice.

TRUTH 7

Abortion Cheapens Human Life

Peter Singer, who served as professor of bioethics at Princeton University from 1999 until 2004, has been hailed by **The New York Times** *as the world's most influential living philosopher.[54] This "ethicist" has publicly argued that parents should have a right to murder their children 28 days* ***after*** *birth.*

When asked, "Would you kill a disabled baby?" Singer responded,

Yes, if that was in the best interests of the baby and of the family as a whole. Many people find this shocking, yet they support a woman's right to have an abortion. One point on which I agree with opponents of abortion is that—from the point of view of ethics rather than the law—there is no sharp distinction between the fetus and the newborn baby.[55]

◢ *Would Kill Disabled Babies: Peter Singer (AP/Wide World)*

Abortion Double Standard

The beliefs of Peter Singer may be repulsive, but at least they are consistent. *There is no sharp distinction between the fetus and the newborn baby.* Singer's view throws light on our cultural double standard. Many people shrug at the issue of abortion, then act horrified when a mother treats her newborn baby like worthless garbage. Who could forget the story of 18-year-old Melissa Drexler, who served three years in prison after throwing her newborn baby in a trash can at her high school prom? During her trial, she confessed:

> I went to the prom and I went into the bathroom and delivered the baby. The baby was born alive. I knowingly took the baby out of the toilet and wrapped a series of garbage bags around the baby.... I was aware of what I was doing at the time when I placed the baby in the bag. And I was further aware that what I did would most certainly result in the death of the baby.[56]

Why is the story of this baby's death any more appalling than the tens of millions of unborn children who have been dismembered, burned, stabbed, decapitated, and thrown into trash bins? Are these lives any less precious, simply because they were snuffed out inside of their mothers' wombs? According to our courts, the answer is yes.

Elizabeth Ehlert gave birth to a six-pound, 19-inch baby girl,[57] wrapped her in a plastic bag, and threw the newborn into a canal behind her house. Her fiancé told police that he heard the baby cry after the delivery, and medical experts testified that they suspected drowning to be the cause of death. Consequently, Ehlert was convicted of murder.

Tortured Logic

However, an Illinois appellate court overturned the conviction—explaining that the law could not consider the baby to be legally "alive" if the umbilical cord had not yet been cut at the time of her death. Thus, the court ruled that the death "may have occurred before complete separation from the mother, and therefore it is not sufficient to prove live birth."[58] In other words, a crying baby has no rights—and is not legally alive—until its umbilical cord has been completely detached from the mother.

In a culture that fails to treasure life, such tortured semantics are offered in a pathetic attempt to justify the most callous of evils. Modern historians ponder how the German people could have allowed the Holocaust to occur right under their noses. Former German President Richard von Weizsaecker, who lived through the Holocaust era, confessed:

There were many ways of not burdening one's conscience, of shunning responsibility, looking away, keeping mum. When the unspeakable truth of the Holocaust then became known at the end of the war, all too many of us claimed that they had not known anything about it or even suspected anything.[59]

◄ *Nazi death camp inmates at Auschwitz. (Newscom)*

Americans can no longer plead ignorance. If our nation is ever to be seen as a beacon of virtue in an increasingly dark world, we must not sit idly by and ignore the violent slaughter of millions of unborn children. We must treasure life from conception to natural death.

TRUTH 8

Abortion Discriminates and Treats the Less Fortunate as Less Valuable.

Ironically, the people who seem so determined to stamp out discrimination of every sort are often the same people who willfully ignore the bigoted and discriminatory nature of the abortion industry. Even a cursory glance at the statistics reveals that a disproportionate number of abortion's victims are minorities, females, and disabled persons. Any abortion—even of a healthy white male baby—is discriminatory. It determines that the small, the weak, the helpless, and the voiceless do not have equal rights with the rest of us.

"Human Weeds"

Two decades before Adolf Hitler attempted to create a "master race," Margaret Sanger, the founder of Planned Parenthood, had already demonstrated her own morbid fascination with eugenics—the Darwinian notion of "improving" the human race through selective breeding. Sanger wrote extensively about her plans for discouraging reproduction among certain peoples in articles with titles like: "Birth Control and Racial Betterment," "Some Moral Aspects of Eugenics," "The Eugenic Conscience," and "The Purpose of Eugenics."[60]

✓ *Margaret Sanger (Getty Hulton Archive)*

Sanger harbored an intense disdain for the less fortunate. "Such human weeds clog up the path, drain up the energies and the resources of this little earth," she wrote. "We must clear the way for a better world; we must cultivate our garden."[61]

Who did Sanger have in mind when she wrote of human weeds? Perhaps this question is best answered by Sanger's own "Negro Project"—a program which she boasted was "helping Negroes to control their birth rate." When African-Americans voiced concerns about the ultimate aspirations of her birth control clinics, Sanger sent a letter to a colleague stating:

> If we can train the Negro doctor at the clinic, he can go among them with enthusiasm and with knowledge, which, I believe, will have far-reaching results.... The minister's work is also important ... We do not want word to go out that we want to exterminate the Negro population, and the minister is the man who can straighten out that idea if it ever occurs.[62]

Blacks Most Affected

The civil rights movement has made tremendous strides since the 1920s, yet Sanger's legacy of death endures. Abortion is now the leading cause of death for black Americans, claiming more than 1,400 African-American lives per day. Joseph Parker is the pastor of Campbell Chapel AME Church in Pulaski, Tennessee, the birthplace of the Ku Klux Klan. He bluntly stated, "Planned Parenthood kills more black people in three days than the Klan has killed in its entire history of existence. Yet many in the African-American community don't even see Planned Parenthood as an enemy; (they) would see them as a friend."[63]

Though black Americans comprise only 12 percent of the U.S. population, black women account for a stunning 29 percent of all abortions in America. The Centers for Disease Control confirmed, "The abortion rate for black women

(29 per 1,000 women) was 3.0 times the rate for white women (10 per 1,000)."[64]

Abortion not only disproportionately targets racial minorities, but it has done immeasurable damage to women. Radical feminists blindly embrace abortion as the cornerstone of the women's rights movement, yet new studies reveal that abortion has decimated the world's female population.

"Missing" Women and Abortion

One international study recently discovered that there are roughly 107 million "missing" women in the world—largely due to gender-selective abortions. "We are confronted by the slaughter of Eve, a systematic gendercide of tragic proportions," said Theodor Winkler, author of the study. "Women live in a very insecure world indeed. Many fall victim to gender selective abortion and infanticide (boys being preferred to girls)."[65]

Too many parents no longer embrace *all* children as a blessing from God and use abortion as a means to "weed out" children with undesirable attributes. Scientists are now debating the ethical implications of creating genetically engineered "designer babies." In Texas, one "embryo bank" allows prospective clients to choose the race, educational background, attractiveness, hair and eye color, and other genetic traits of sperm and egg donors before purchasing embryos.

In a society consumed with external appearance, the less fortunate are seen as less valuable. Thus, unborn babies diagnosed with genetic disorders or physical abnormalities are far more likely to be killed in the womb.

One study revealed that roughly ninety percent of pregnant women whose baby is given a Down Syndrome diagnosis choose abortion.[66]

In an editorial in *The Washington Post,* Patricia Bauer, whose daughter has Down Syndrome, offered this chilling comparison:

> "In ancient Greece, babies with disabilities were left out in the elements to die. We in America rely on prenatal genetic testing to make our selections in private, but the effect on society is the same."

MANY AMERICANS ARE INTENT ON PLAYING GOD RATHER THAN TRUSTING GOD.

Most Americans have seen the remarkable photograph of an unborn baby reaching from the womb and grabbing a surgeon's finger. That baby was Samuel Armas, who was diagnosed in the womb with spina bifida. Thankfully, Samuel's mother refused to abort God's gift of life. "Abortion is wrong," she said. "Life in the womb is God-created, even with birth defects. God doesn't make mistakes, whether creating a child with spina bifida, Down syndrome, or even more severe issues. It is still a life that has just as much a right to live as any 'normal' unborn child."[67]

▶ **Samuel Armas**
God's gift of life.

© *Michael Clancy*

TRUTH 9

The Bible Declares the Truth About Abortion

The Bible, God's Word, is not silent on abortion.

The Bible teaches us that life is to be treasured, and children—who are "the fruit of the womb" and "a heritage from the Lord"—are to be cherished as a blessing from God. Jesus, Himself, displayed tremendous love for young children and infants during His earthly ministry. "Let the little children come to Me," He commanded His disciples, "and do not forbid them; for of such is the kingdom of God."[68]

Luke's Gospel tells us that people brought their "infants" to Him.[69] The Greek word used by Luke for "infants" is *brephos*. When the Gospel of Luke tells of Jesus in the manger, Jesus is called a *brephos*.[70] When Luke describes an unborn baby leaping in the womb, he uses the same word: *brephos*.[71] The Bible makes no distinction between born and unborn. The Greek word *brephos* is used interchangeably to describe them both.

The Bible is Clear

Scripture leaves no room for doubt about the moral status of the unborn. Pregnant women are said to be "with child." God does not see the unborn as clumps of tissue without purpose or value. The Scriptures make this abundantly clear!

In the Psalms, the Holy Spirit inspired King David to pray:

O Lord ... You formed my inward parts;

You covered me in my mother's womb.
I will praise You, for I am fearfully and
wonderfully made; marvelous are Your
works, and that my soul knows very well.
My frame was not hidden from
You, when I was made in secret, and
skillfully wrought in the lowest parts of
the earth. Your eyes saw my substance,
being yet unformed. And in Your book they
all were written, the days fashioned for
me, when as yet there were none of them.

—Psalm 139:13-16

The Lord declares to Jeremiah:

> Before I formed you in the womb I knew
> you; before you were born I sanctified you.
>
> —Jeremiah 1:5

Job, the great hero of patient suffering, said,

> Did not He who made me in the womb
> make them? Did not the same One fashion
> us in the womb?
>
> —Job 31:15

The prophet Isaiah proclaimed,

> Thus says the Lord who made you and
> formed you from the womb...
>
> —Isaiah 44:2

The Bible offers dignity to the unborn not only in poetic tribute, but through legal protections. When God delivered His law to the people of Israel through the prophet Moses, He specified that unborn children are not of lesser worth. They are to be given the same rights as those who are already born.

> If men fight, and hurt a woman with child, so that she gives birth prematurely, yet no harm follows, he shall surely be punished accordingly as the woman's husband imposes on him; and he shall pay as the judges determine. But if any harm follows, then you shall give life for life …
> —Exodus 21:22-23

The sixth commandment declares, "You shall not murder,"[72] and the Law of Moses specifies that "if anyone kills a person, the murderer shall be put to death."[73] By including the murder of an unborn baby in the list of capital crimes ("life for life"), the Bible is explicitly treating unborn children with the same dignity and value as the most developed of adults.

Created in His Image

All human life is given extraordinary value, because it is created in the image of God.[74] Thus, an attack on human life is an attack upon the image of God Himself. In Proverbs, this connection is made when God proclaims, "All those who hate Me love death."[75]

The people of God are to cherish life. In centuries past, a barren womb was a thing to be feared. Today, it seems that people go out of their way to avoid children. People sympathetic to abortion have argued that abortion is a necessary evil to prevent undue hardship and overpopulation; how different is the perspective of a Christian, who sees the world through eyes of faith.

> Behold, children are a heritage from the Lord, the fruit of the womb is a reward. Like arrows in the hand of a warrior, so are the children of one's youth. Happy is the man who has his quiver full of them; they shall not be ashamed, but shall speak with their enemies in the gate.
> —Psalm 127:3-5

The Lord is not ambiguous about bringing children into the world. Twice He commands:

Be fruitful and multiply.
—Genesis 1:28 and Genesis 9:7

Abortion is a perversion of this command and a rejection of God's gift of life and family. No matter who you are, all people are called to stand in defense of life.

> Open your mouth for the speechless, in the cause of all who are appointed to die.
> —Proverbs 31:8

Ending Infanticide

The Word of God must be the primary weapon in the Church's battle against abortion. In the past, the Bible has changed societies' perceptions about abortion. Fifteen-hundreds years ago, as the Christianity spread throughout the West, the ancient Greek and Roman practices of infanticide were abandoned and finally outlawed by Emperor Justinian. The Justinian Code declared,

> **Those who expose children, possibly hoping they would die, and those who use the potions of the abortionist, are subject to the full penalty of the law—both civil and ecclesiastical—for murder. Should exposure occur, the finder of the child is to see that he is baptized and that he is treated with Christian care and compassion. They may be then adopted as *ad scriptitiorum*— even as we ourselves have been adopted into the kingdom of grace.[76]**

Christians are called to be Christ-like. Surely, no person in history has demonstrated a greater zeal and passion for the life of His people than Jesus Christ. Can we who claim the name of Christ do anything less? Can we ignore the clear command of Scripture?

> Rescue those being led away to death;
> hold back those staggering toward
> slaughter. If you say, "But we knew
> nothing about this,"does not he who
> weighs the heart perceive it?
> Does not he who guards your life know it?
> Will he not repay each person according
> to what he has done?
> —Proverbs 24:11-12

TRUTH 10

There Is Healing and Forgiveness for Women Who Have Had Abortions

Some women, confronted with the terrible realization that they are responsible for the death of their own child, may ask despairingly, "How could God ever forgive me for killing my baby?"

The Bible embraces them with tender words of healing grace:

> God demonstrates His own love toward us,
> in that while we were still sinners, Christ
> died for us.
>
> —Romans 5:8

No sin can eclipse the mercy of God; no person is beyond the reach of God's redemptive love.

King David, a man well acquainted with God's amazing grace, wrote:

> Bless the Lord, O my soul,
> and forget not all His benefits:
> Who forgives all your iniquities,
> who heals all your diseases,
> Who redeems your life
> from destruction,
> Who crowns you with loving
> kindness and tender mercies ...
> He has not dealt with us
> according to our sins,
> Nor punished us according
> to our iniquities.
> For as the heavens are

high above the earth,
So great is His mercy
toward those who fear Him;
As far as the east is from the west,
So far has He removed our
transgressions from us.

—Psalm 103:2-4, 10-12

Mercy for Sinners

God is *not* some stern cosmic judge, sitting in Heaven and waiting to punish those who transgress His holy standards of righteousness. He does not treat us as our sins deserve. God is our loving heavenly Father, who redeems our lives and crowns us with love and mercy.

Yet Scripture *does* clearly assert that we are not capable of measuring up to God's standard of perfection on our own. The Apostle John wrote, "If we say that we have not sinned, we make Him a liar, and His Word is not in us."[77] The Bible contains awful, ominous news for all mankind:

There is none righteous, no, not one;
There is none who understands;
There is none who seeks after God.
They have all turned aside;
They have together
become unprofitable;
There is none who does good,
no, not one.

—Romans 3:10–12

The Bible's solemn bottom line: "All have sinned and fall short of the glory of God."[78] The Epistle to the Romans bluntly warns, "The wages of sin is death."[79] In other words, no one is capable of standing guiltless before God based on his or her own righteousness. Everyone, from the church deacon to the mass murderer on death row, is in need of a redeemer. We are all unworthy of God's kind affection, yet Jesus came to save us from death and to endure the full punishment for our iniquity. Jesus declared,

> I have come that they may have life, and
> that they may have it more abundantly.
> I am the good shepherd. The good
> shepherd gives His life for the sheep.
> —John 10:10-11

The Apostle Paul once hated Christians with a cruel fury that few could match. "I persecuted this Way to the death," he candidly admitted, "binding and delivering into prisons both men and women."[80] Then Paul encountered Jesus Christ, and his life was forever changed, and his complete confidence in God's absolute forgiveness gives joyous hope to all who come to Christ in faith:

> **For I am persuaded that neither death
> nor life, nor angels nor principalities nor
> powers, nor things present nor things to
> come, nor height nor depth, nor any other
> created thing, shall be able to separate
> us from the love of God which is in Christ
> Jesus our Lord.**
>
> **—Romans 8:38-39**

Like Paul, countless post-abortive women have found healing and forgiveness beneath the Cross of Jesus.

Beauty for Ashes

At age eighteen, Tewannah Aman aborted her first child. Plagued by guilt, she later received Christ's forgiveness. Several years later she married and became pregnant, but lost the baby after a premature delivery—caused by a complication from her abortion. Today, she has devoted her life to helping women and saving other unborn children. "I miss my children," she admits, "but God is using what I've gone through to save babies and to minister to others who are hurting and who need to know that there's hope in Christ."

↗ *Tewannah Aman*

Another woman stated, "Someday I will meet my son, David, in heaven. Just as Jesus still bears the scars of the cross, my scars remain. But God has turned the pain into a thing which can bring glory to Him and lead others to forgiveness."[81]

The Prophet Isaiah tells us that the Lord seeks to "provide for those who grieve ... to bestow on them a crown of beauty instead of ashes, the oil of gladness instead of mourning, and a garment of praise instead of a spirit of despair."[82]

Norma McCorvey (the "Roe" of *Roe v. Wade*) faced unimaginable burdens of guilt, mourning, and despair. After all, it was her case that paved the way for an atrocity that has slaughtered tens of millions of babies. Yet after a sweet eight-year-old girl named Emily gently pleaded, "You don't have to go to hell, Miss Norma. You can pray right now and Jesus will forgive you," McCorvey recalls, "This childlike faith cut open my heart."

McCorvey agreed to come to church, where she heard a sermon on John 3:16—***"For God so loved the world that He gave His only begotten Son, that whoever believes in Him should not perish but have everlasting life."***

Norma McCorvey then surrendered her life to Christ. She later wrote,

> It made me feel so incredibly sorry for all my sins, especially for my role in legalizing abortion. I just kept repeating over and over, "I just want to undo all the evil I've done in this world. I'm so sorry, God. I'm so, so sorry...." Finally, I stopped crying and broke into the biggest smile of my life. I no longer felt the pressure of my sin pushing down on my shoulders.... [Today], I'm one hundred percent sold out to Jesus and one hundred percent pro-life.[83]

Today, "Miss Norma" stands as a magnificent trophy of God's amazing grace.

You, too, can be sheltered in the arms of God's love and forgiveness. The Scriptures promise, "If we confess our sins, He is faithful and just to forgive us our sins and to cleanse us from all unrighteousness."[84]

You may think your past cannot be pardoned but if you come to Jesus you will find that He is a tender and merciful Savior. He is God in human flesh and took the punishment for our sins when He died on the cross. Now He offers you forgiveness and the wonderful promise that "... whoever comes to me, I will never drive away" (John 6:37 NIV).

Jesus has already shown that
He loves you to death.
If you come to Him, Jesus can love you to life!

ENDNOTES

1   **Dr. D. James Kennedy,** "Turning Back the Clock," WorldNetDaily, January 20, 2005.
    http://www.worldnetdaily.com/news/article.asp?ARTICLE_ID=42466

2   **"Support for Abortion in Sharp Decline,"** Zogby Poll, January 23, 2006.
    http://www.zogby.com/news/ReadNews2.dbm?ID=1060

3   **Elizabeth Armet,** "Poll Analysis: Americans Lean More Conservative on Social Issues,"
    Los Angeles Times, June 18, 2000. http://www.latimes.com/news/nationworld/timespoll
    /la-000618abortpoll-442pa2an,1,7894326.htmlstory?coll=la-news-times_poll-nation

4   **Chris McComb,** "Teens Lean Conservative on Abortion," The Gallup Poll, November 18, 2003.
    http://www.galluppoll.com/content/?ci=9715

5   **"Conscience, Religion Alter How Doctors Tell Patients About Options,"**
    University of Chicago Medical Center, February 7, 2007.
    http://www.uchospitals.edu/news/2007/20070207-ethics.html

6   **William Mears and Bob Franken,** "30 Years After Ruling, Ambiguity, Anxiety Surround
    Abortion Debate," *CNN News*, January 22, 2003.
    http://www.cnn.com/2003/LAW/01/21/roevwade.overview/

7   **"Access to Abortion,"** National Abortion Federation, 2003.
    http://www.prochoice.org/pubs_research/publications/downloads/about_abortion
    /access_abortion.pdf

8   **Naseem Sowti,** "Abortion: Just the Data," *The Washington Post*, July 19, 2005.
    http://www.washingtonpost.com/wp-dyn/content/article/2005/07/18/AR2005071801164.html

9   **Dr. D. James Kennedy,** "Abortion: Myths and Realities," October 28, 1984.

10 **Fred de Miranda,** MD, FCP, "Position Statements: When Human Life Begins,"
    American College of Pediatricians, March 17, 2004.
    http://acpeds.org/?CONTEXT=art&cat=10007&art=53&BISKIT=2170483

11 **Leonard Peikoff,** "Abortion Rights Are Pro-Life," Ayn Rand Institute, January 17, 2003.
    http://www.aynrand.org/site/News2?page=NewsArticle&id=7893

12 *Roe v. Wade*, 410 U.S. 113, Supreme Court of the United States, January 22, 1973.

13 **Report,** Subcommittee on Separation of Powers to Senate Judiciary Committee
    S-158, 97 Congress, 1st Session 1981, p. 7.

14 **McArthur Hill, M.D.,** "Meet the Abortion Providers," Pro-Life Action League, February 1989.
    http://www.prolifeaction.org/providers/hill.htm

15 **David Kupelian,** "Innocent blood: How lying marketers sold *Roe v. Wade* to America,"
    WorldNetDaily, January 20, 2005.
    http://www.worldnetdaily.com/news/article.asp?ARTICLE_ID=42462

16   ***Gonzales v. Carhart***, No. 05-380, Supreme Court of the United States, April 18, 2007.
      http://www.supremecourtus.gov/opinions/06pdf/05-380.pdf

17   **Carol Everett**, "Meet the Abortion Providers," Pro-Life Action Network, November 1987.
      http://www.prolifeaction.org/providers/everett.htm

18   ***Gonzales v. Carhart***, No. 05-380, Supreme Court of the United States, April 18, 2007.
      http://www.supremecourtus.gov/opinions/06pdf/05-380.pdf

19   **Senator Sam Brownback**, "Unborn Child Pain Awareness Act,"
      Congressional Record, Volume 151, No. 6; January 26, 2005.
      http://www.priestsforlife.org/government/brownback05-01-26unbornpain.pdf

20   **"Pain of the Unborn,"** National Right to Life Educational Trust Fund, September 2004.
      http://www.nrlc.org/abortion/Fetal_Pain/FetalPain091604.pdf

21   **Senator Sam Brownback**, "Unborn Child Pain Awareness Act," January 22, 2007.
      http://brownback.senate.gov/english/legissues/cultureoflife/unbornchildpainact.cfm

22   **Reprinted** from online reproduction of video script at http://www.silentscream.org/silent_e.htm

23   **"Operation Outcry,"** The Justice Foundation, Julie Thomas.
      http://www.operationoutcry.org/pages.asp?pageid=29197

24   **1. "Induced Abortion and Traumatic Stress,"** *Medical Science Monitor*, 2004.
      http://www.medscimonit.com/pub/vol_10/no_10/4923.pdf
      2. "Possible Effects of Abortion," Physicians for Life, October 2005.
      http://www.physiciansforlife.org/content/view/75/50/
      3. Karen Malec, "The Abortion-Breast Cancer Link: How Politics Trumped Science and Informed
      Consent," *Journal of American Physicians and Surgeons*, Volume VIII, Number 2, Summer 2003.
      http://www.jpands.org/vol8no2/malec.pdf
      4. David C. Reardon, Ph.D., "List of Major Physical Sequelae Related to Abortion,"
      Elliot Institute, 1997.http://www.abortionfacts.com/reardon/effect_of_abortion.asp

25   **"Choosing Abortion,"** Planned Parenthood Federation of America, 2006.

26   **Dr. Anthony Levatino**, "Meet the Abortion Providers," Pro-Life Action League, speech given in
      Chicago, Illinois, November 1987. http://www.priestsforlife.org/testimony/levatinolong.htm

27   **David Reardon**, Philip G. Ney, Fritz J. Scheuren, Jesse R. Cougle, Priscilla K. Coleman, Thomas
      W. Stahan, "Suicide Deaths Associated With Pregnancy Outcome," First World Congress on Women's
      Mental Health, March 27-31, 2001. http://clinmed.netprints.org/cgi/content/full/2001030003v1

28   **"Report of the South Dakota Task Force to Study Abortion,"**
      South Dakota Task Force to Study Abortion, December 2005.

29   **"Academy Award winning actress Ellen Burstyn** Says Abortion was the Worst Thing in Her
      Life," LifeSiteNews.com, September 2007.

30   ***Gonzales v. Carhart***, No. 05-380, Supreme Court of the United States, April 18, 2007.
      http://www.supremecourtus.gov/opinions/06pdf/05-380.pdf

31   **Brief of Sandra Cano and 180 Women Injured by Abortion**,
           Gonzales v. Carhart, No. 05-380, August 12, 2003.
           http://www.thejusticefoundation.org/images/64456/Gonzalesv.Carhart-AmicusBrief.pdf

32   **Ibid.**

33   **David Kupelian,** *Marketing of Evil*, Cumberland House Publishing,
           Nashville, Tennessee, 2005, p.191.

34   **Dr. D. James Kennedy,** "Lies and More Lies," Coral Ridge Ministries, 2003.

35   **Dr. Bernard Nathanson,** *The Hand of God: A Journey from Death to Life*, "Confession of an Ex-
           Abortionist," 1997.

36   **"In Abortion Debate**, It's Time to Say We're Sorry," *Jewish World Review*, June 20, 2001.
           http://www.jewishworldreview.com/kathleen/parker062001.asp

37   *Affidavit of Sandra Cano, Donna Santa Marie v. Christine Todd Whitman*, Civil Action No.
           99-2692, March 15, 2000. http://www.eadshome.com/DoeAffidavit.htm

38   *McCorvey v. Hill*, No. 03-10711, Fifth U.S. Circuit Court of Appeals, September 14, 2004.
           ftp://opinions.ca5.uscourts.gov/byDate/Sep2004/Sep20/03-10711-CV0.wpd.pdf

39   **Antonin Scalia** (concurring opinion), *Ohio v. Akron Center*, No. 88-805, U.S. Supreme Court,
           June 25, 1990.
           http://www.law.cornell.edu/supct/html/88-805.ZC1.html

40   **Senator John Cornyn,** "Liberal Criticisms of Roe," November 15, 2005.
           http://www.cornyn.senate.gov/record.cfm?id=248771

41   **"The Supreme Court**, 1972 Term—Foreword: Toward a Model of Roles in the Due Process of Life
           and Law," 87 *Harvard Law Review* 1, 7 (1973).

42   **Edward Lazarus**, "The Lingering Problems With *Roe v. Wade*, and Why the Recent Senate
           Hearings on Michael McConnell's Nomination Only Underlined Them," October 3, 2002.
           http://writ.corporate.findlaw.com/lazarus/20021003.html

43   **"The Cost of Abortion**," The Guttmacher Institute, 2007.
           http://www.guttmacher.org/in-the-know/cost.html

44   **David Kupelian**, *Marketing of Evil*, Cumberland House Publishing,
           Nashville, Tennessee, 2005, p.198.

45   **"Meet the Abortion Providers,"** Carol Everett, Pro-Life Action League, November 1987.
           http://www.prolifeaction.org/providers/everett.htm

46   **"An Interview with Norma McCorvey, the 'Roe' of *Roe vs. Wade*,"** Priests for Life, 1997.
           http://www.priestsforlife.org/testimony/normapflinterview.htm

47   **David Kupelian**, *Marketing of Evil*, Cumberland House Publishing,
           Nashville, Tennessee, 2005, p. 195.

48   **"Planned Parenthood Annual Report 2005-2006,"**
      Planned Parenthood Federation of America, June 30, 2006.
      http://www.plannedparenthood.org/files/PPFA/Annual_report.pdf

49   **Dr. Kelly Hollowell,** *Struggling for Life*, Coral Ridge Ministries, January 2006.

50   **"Detailed Service Data for Planned Parenthood's last 5 Years,"** STOPP International, 2001.
      http://www.all.org/stopp/sdlast5y.htm

51   **"WISQARS Leading Causes of Death Reports 1999-2004,"** Centers for Disease Control and
      Prevention, 2004. http://webappa.cdc.gov/sasweb/ncipc/leadcaus10.html

52   **"Cancer Facts & Figures 2004,"** American Cancer Society, 2004.
      http://www.cancer.org/downloads/STT/CAFF_finalPWSecured.pdf

53   **"Public Funding for Abortion: Medicaid and the Hyde Amendment,"**
      National Abortion Federation, 2006.
      http://www.prochoice.org/pubs_research/publications/downloads/about_abortion/public_funding.pdf

54   **J.B. Schneewind, "Don't Bring Home the Bacon,"** *The New York Times*, December 17, 2000.
      http://www.nytimes.com/books/00/12/17/reviews/001217.17schneet.html?_r=1&oref=slogin

55   **"Peter Singer: You Ask the Questions,"** *The Independent*, September 11, 2006.
      http://news.independent.co.uk/people/profiles/article1466409.ece

56   **" 'Prom Mom' Admits Killing Newborn,"** *CNN*, August 20, 1998.
      http://www.cnn.com/US/9808/20/prom.birth.02/

57   **Jill Stanek,** "When A Crying Baby Is Not Alive," *WorldNetDaily*, October 3, 2003.
      http://www.worldnetdaily.com/news/article.asp?ARTICLE_ID=34900

58   ***People v. Elizabeth Ehlert***, No. 1-00-0273, Appeal from the Circuit court of Cook County, Judge
      Karen Thompson Tobin Presiding, November 18, 2002.
      http://www.state.il.us/court/OPINIONS/AppellateCourt/2002/1stDistrict/November/Wp/1000273.doc

59   **Carl Schweitzer,** *Politics and Government in Germany 1944-1994*, Berghahn Books,
      Providence, Rhode Island, 1995, p. 267.

60   **"The Truth About Margaret Sanger,"** Planned Parenthood Federation of America, 2006.
      http://www.plannedparenthood.org/files/PPFA/fact-margaret-sanger.pdf.

61   **"The Need of Birth Control in America,"** in *Birth Control: Facts and Responsibilities*, edited by
      Adolf Meyer, The Williams and Wilkins Co., Baltimore, 1925, pp. 47-48.

62   **"The Truth About Margaret Sanger,"** Planned Parenthood Federation of America, 2006.

63   **"Abortion is No. 1 Killer in Black Community,"** Focus on the Family Action CitizenLink.com,
      August 7, 2007. http://www.citizenlink.com/CLBriefs/A000005214.cfm

64   **"Abortion Surveillance—United States, 2002,"** Centers for Disease Control: Division of
      Reproductive Health. http://www.cdc.gov/mmwr/preview/mmwrhtml/ss5407a1.htm

65   **Theodor H. Winkler**, "Women in an Insecure World: Executive Summary," Geneva Centre for the Democratic Control of Armed Forces, January 2007.

66   **Amy Harmon**, "Prenatal Test Puts Down Syndrome in Hard Focus," *The New York Times*, May 9, 2007.
http://www.nytimes.com/2007/05/09/us/09down.html
?ex=1336363200&en=ccf8eef18ff478e4&ei=5088&partner=r

67   **J. Gerald Harris**, "Beyond Spina Bifida: Samuel & Zachary Are Answers to Prayer," Southern Baptist Press, January 20, 2006.
http://www.sbcbaptistpress.org/bpnews.asp?ID=22487

68   **Luke 18:16**

69   **Luke 18:17**

70   **Luke 2:16**

71   **Luke 1:41**

72   **Exodus 20:13**

73   **Number 35:30**

74   **Genesis 1:27**

75   **Proverbs 8:36b**

76   **D. James Kennedy and Jerry Newcombe**, *What If Jesus Had Never Been Born?*, Thomas Nelson Publishers, Nashville, Tennessee, 1994, p. 11.

77   **1 John 1:10**

78   **Romans 3:23**

79   **Romans 6:23**

80   **Acts 22:4**

81   **"Post-Abortive Case #744,"** Priests for Life, 2007.

82   **Isaiah 61:3**

83   **Norma McCorvey**, "*Roe v. McCorvey*," January 1998.
http://www.leaderu.com/norma/nmtestimony.html

84   **1 John 1:9**

TAKE THE NEXT STEP!

Go online at www.coralridge.org and click the Equip and Grow tab, where you can:

"Face the Opposition." Watch the online video and see if you can answer actual pro-abortion arguments.

Download talking points for the Ten Truths About Abortion.

Download the Ten Truths About Abortion PowerPoint presentation. Perfect to share with your small group or Sunday school class.

Request the gripping video version of Ten Truths About Abortion on DVD.

Select additional pro-life resources.